As Within So Without

Everything is Interconnected

Shruti Tiwari

BookLeaf Publishing

India | USA | UK

Made with ❤ on the BookLeaf Publishing Platform
www.bookleafpub.in
www.bookleafpub.com

Dedication

For those who wander through the shadows of their hearts,

And find light in the whispered verses of their souls.

To the dreamers, the seekers, and the storytellers,

May these words inspire your journey,

And remind you that every fleeting moment

Holds the power to become a timeless poem.

With love and gratitude,

I dedicate this collection to you.

Preface

In the quiet moments of life, when the world seems to pause, poetry often emerges as a refuge—a space where words dance and emotions intertwine. This collection is born from a tapestry cf experiences, reflections, and revelations, woven together in the hopes of capturing the essence of what it means to be human.

Each poem is a glimpse into the heart's landscape, revealing the beauty of jcy, the pain of loss, and the quiet strength found in vulnerability. These verses are inspired by fleeting moments, intricate relationships, and the natural world around us. They are whispers of truth echoing against the backdrop of our existence, inviting us to slow down and listen to the stories that shape us.

Writing this collection has been a journey of exploration and self-discovery. Each piece represents a step along a winding path, illuminating the highs and lows we navigate in our daily lives. Here, you will find both solace and challenge, an invitation to reflect on your own experiences as you traverse the delicate terrain of life alongside me.

I hope these poems resonate with you in some way, providing comfort in times of uncertainty or inspiration during moments of clarity. As you read, I encourage you to seek your own meanings, to let your imagination run free, and to discover the layers of emotion hidden within the lines.

Thank you for joining me on this journey through words, and may you find within these pages a glimmer of connection, understanding, and perhaps even a piece of yourself.

With warmth and sincerity,
Shruti Tiwari

Acknowledgements

Creating this collection of poetry has been a deeply personal journey, and I am filled with gratitude for the countless individuals who have supported me along the way.

First and foremost, I would like to thank my family and friends, whose unwavering love and encouragement have been my guiding light. Your belief in my voice has inspired me to put pen to paper and embrace my creativity without fear.

To my fellow poets and mentors, thank you for sharing your wisdom, passion, and artistry. Your insights have challenged me to grow and have enriched my understanding of the poetic form.

A heartfelt thank you to the readers who take the time to engage with my words. Your openness to literature and poetry fuels my desire to write and share my experiences. I hope that these pages resonate with you and spark your own reflections.

Finally, I owe a debt of gratitude to the creative community—publishers, editors, and artists—who bring these words to life. Your expertise and dedication have turned a collection of verses into a tangible reality.

Every poem in this book carries with it a bit of your spirit, and for that, I am eternally thankful. May we continue to celebrate the beauty of language together.

With all my appreciation,
Shruti Tiwari

1. That Girl

They kept pushing her towards the darkness,
Inane & thoughtless ones thought;
That she'll be weak & frail and would give up.
But they forgot that,
The same darkness was filled with moon light which
gave her powers;
As she was the kind of girl that had been making wishes
on the
full moon.

2. Blinded by Love

She didn't know where to stop,
Once she started to give in.
She just kept doing it for others,
Thinking only about them.
Wondering where is she going wrong?

She was so innocent and genuine at heart,
That she just kept getting trampled on by them.
She had a big heart and only chose to see good in them.
So, she didn't know when to stop giving in.
Wondering where is she going wrong?

Until one day when her tears went dry,
Her heart exhausted.
She yet didn't know how to give up on people,
Who burned holes in her heart.
Wondering if it was better to be blind in the eye rather
than to be blinded by love.

3. The Baffling Stillness

The eagles hovering over in the sky,
It was a windless afternoon;
The leaves didn't rustle,
The afternoon felt seemingly quiet.

Everything seemed still in the balmy Summer days,
The calmness was like her still life.
Whatever she did tested her patience,
It made her weary.

The anxiousness of the unexpected had hit her life.
She was used to chaos to such extent
That the tranquility shook her core.
As though her wild soul was on tenterhooks.

Life had its own course lately,
She would barely get to navigate her ship.
The divine intervention and timing baffled her.
She was left wondering is it calm before the storm or is it
like a watched pot that never boils?...

4. The One

Entering the unknown territory,
I see a part of me which I thought was my identity.
Treading into the uncharted, I realised that this is not
me...
Since years I'm just versions of what they made me.
But here into the unknown...
I am lesser than even a speck of dust...
I am no one here...
This is the reality...
Now when I see myself as nothing is when I see the real
self.
I go back in reverse and unbecome my versions...
Finding the one in myself...

5. Feel Like 'You' Again..

Cut those parts of you where they yet reside,
Those residues need to be released;
Or else you'll just keep feeling heavy and stagnant.

When you try to overcome those heavy latching feelings,
It gives them the power to suck on your happiness like a
leech.
This can happen even though they aren't physically
around.
So, shed those parts which resonate to them.

Release it off your system!
Once you do it, you'll metamorphose!
You'll cry and laugh and dance at the same time!
This release is important to your well being and to revive
your sanity.

And most importantly, it'll help you to connect to your
inner child again.
There's no other feeling like this in the world...

It'll feel like 'you' again but in a new light!
Rebirth dear, REBIRTH!!

6. The Love You Deserve

The love you crave is the love that you give others.
Unconditional love,
Unfiltered love,
The love that desires you.
The love that understands every thing that you do,
The love that understands every little gesture of yours,
The love that won't be able to gulp a morsel when you're
starving.
The love who is as crazy about you as you are,
The love where you get affected when they're unhappy,
The love where you go to lengths and breadths just to
see them happy.
The love where you don't have to keep giving efforts and
it's misunderstood,
The love that is effortless and not burdensome,
The love that understands your inner child wounds;
The love that helps you heal them.
The love where you feel as gay as a puppy when it finds
the owner.
The moment you have that love that you kept pouring

for others,
Is the moment you realise the reason it didn't work out
with anyone else;
It's the moment you know the love you deserve.

7. Mind vs Heart

Heart: Why are you looking for an answer?
Mind: So that you don't trap yourself once again
Heart: I don't want an answer to why things have
happened... I just want the pain to stay...
Mind: Why would you do that to yourself? Do you like
to suffer?
Heart: That pain is the only thing that I have left of that
person...

8. Letter from Your Higher Version

Whatever has given you the biggest challenge,
Has also been given to you because you can vanquish it
and emerge victorious.
Maybe you're the most courageous and the bravest,
Maybe it is asking you to just move out of your own
bubble that you're trapped in.
Move, my love... Move!
Maybe a few fixes in your life will make you
uncomfortable but to reach somewhere you need to be
eligible too.
That will happen only if you change!
Like when you want to look at your best, you alter your
clothes to your fitting...
Similarly, certain alterations in life may carve a path for
your highest good.
So don't hesitate to embrace the change.
After all, nothing good came out of being in the same
place, isn't it? Then change your direction or location.
Hey! But be kinder to yourself.. okay?

Changes are difficult and you can feel a bit bitter inside.
But don't be hard on yourself.
It's you vs the challenge and not you vs you.
Nothing else matters my love. Embrace the change.
Move closer to your higher version.
Awaiting in anticipation.

Yours truly,
Your Higher Version

9. You're Maa Saraswati and also Maa Kali

With salty tears and moonlit eyes,
She weaves her story wise.
Adrift from the noise,
Her inner self now conspires;
To avenge the ones who threw her in mires.

As she is the one who brings calmness and peace like
Maa Saraswati and Maa Ganga,
Helping the world function.
But she can also bring violence to destroy the evil and
cruel like Maa Bhairavi and Maa Samhara Kali,
Helping the world reform and reconstruct.

The scarier times are here and the rise of evil has begun...
Indeed this rises a question on your existence!
You, the women of India!
You chose to be Saraswati and Ganga to create life and
nurture it...

When will you choose to be Bhairavi and Kali to retaliate
for your kind & save your life & respect?!

10. Nature's Child

The sun hugged her warmly even on darkest days,
The moon listened to all her qualms and her whispers.
The birds and animals surrounded her as they were
awestruck of her,
The magic of nature had slowly began to engulf her.
The magic that she sought outwards was now within her,
Forgetting that she was nature's child.

11. The World is a Reflection

When you have it all backward,
And nothing seems to go forward;
Your patience is being tested the most,
But you have to keep faith in yourself.

Things keep slipping away & there's no control on
anything,
And you leave it all to the above.
You might have no option but to surrender.
It's when you have to have your faith in your beliefs.

The magic begins at the end of the darkest,
You don't seek things outside anymore because you
know it's all a reflection.
Everything happening outwards is mirroring inside too.
As it's all about the inward and it's always been;
That's where you find yourself truly and unravel
different parts.

And amidst all the pandemonium outside,

You start seeking peace inside first.
As you start to become the game changer,
You begin to change the narrative.

Here's where the alchemy sets in,
Leading you to become detached with materials.
Nature becomes more intriguing,
As your soul finds solace in it and resonates to it.

As now you start to see and feel it in your being,
That it's all connected... All of the universe...
As inward so outward,
As above so below.

12. Accept Your Parts

Accept the parts of you that fumbled
Accept the parts of you that stumbled
Accept the parts of you that got embarrassed
Accept the parts of you that was insulted
Accept the parts of you that messed up
Accept the parts of you that failed you
Accept the parts of you that got stomped on
Accept the parts of you that went unnoticed
Accept the parts of you that was disowned
Accept the parts of you that sank down
Accept the parts of you that couldn't save you
Accept & accumulate all of those forgotten parts in your
little self curled up in the desolated state.
Embrace them all and own them!

13. Lost but Found

And whenever she ventured into the woods,
She would vanish into the zone of unknown.
Of unending vastness which was a sight to behold,
She would lose herself but would find some of her parts
too.
The parts that needed to be found,
That she didnt even know were lost;
Until she faced a grave tragedy,
But now she could be herself here, she felt it in her
bones.
As she sees hope in blooming flower and fascinating sky,
She was mesmerized with nature as the rats were with
the Pied Piper.
She felt the euphoria in the lap of nature,
This feeling she hadn't felt in ages.
She left the worldly pleasures to be with her kind,
Only to be lost but to be found.

14. Light & Dark

They say that darkness is scary,
But funnily don't fret their own shadows dreary.
Do they run away from their shadows?
Do they run away from themselves?

For darkness is mere absence of light,
Both are just sides of the same coin, right?
Does light and dark run away from each other?
Do they run away from their own essence?

They forget that a star cannot exist without the dark,
Just like the daylight cannot exist without the night.
Does a star run away from darkness?
Does the day run away from the night?

For light is to be revered and appreciated,
While darkness should be accepted and be made peace
with.
Don't be too attached to the bright light for long time or
you won't know what to do with the dark at dusk.

Don't be too attached to the darkest night for long time
or you won't know what to do with the light at dawn.

15. Be the One Who Keeps You Happy

Our society teaches us that taking care of ourselves first is selfish and a bad thing.

Growing up, I've realized that's one of the most absurd things to teach.

You need to prioritize yourself first and then care for others.

You can't be pouring into other cups and just keep starving yourself of the love and care you need first.

Taking care of yourself is keeping your cup full.

If you don't do things to keep your cup full, you have nothing left to give or share with others or even with yourself.

I feel this tends to be a tough concept for most women.

We've been programmed genetically and socially to be the caregivers, to put others first.

We think we don't deserve to take care of ourselves until everyone else is happy.

Guess what... Everyone will never be happy with you.
It's a pointless quest that does nothing but suck the life
out of us.
Also, keeping yourself happy is only your responsibility
and nobody else's.
Don't burden others with your responsibility.
So, be the one who keeps you happy.

16. Don't Let Your Inner Child Die

The experiences that we have as children, both bad and
good, can significantly impact our lives as we grow up.
Negative or traumatic childhood experiences tend to
stick with us.
We carry this wounded younger self within our adult self
which affects our inner child.
Even though we may not be consciously aware of the
pain our inner child is carrying,
It may be impacting our mental health and relationships.

Many people who experienced hardships growing up
with a "wounded inner child" need healing.
This is where inner child work comes in – the practice of
healing our inner child.
Healing our wounded inner child can help us thrive as
an adult.
We shouldn't let our inner child die.

17. Emotionally Resilient Not Emotionally Reactive

When you feel extremely upset and disappointed,
The situation or problem starts to consume you,
Don't panic and get dismayed by it and run away.

Situations aren't bigger than us,
This happens as we let the emotions take charge of us,
Let the monkey mind take charge of everything
completely.

But when you consider yourself larger than the situation,
You can mentally step outside of it,
Yet there will be problems to be solved;
Yet you will need to take action.

But you need to understand that the chaos is happening
externally.
You are still in the driver's seat internally.
You should take control of the situations.
Do not let the moment or situations control you.

18. Going With the Flow

Going with the flow,
Since a while in a row.
They say its the best thing to follow,
Though its filled with unknown and leaves in limbo;
Most of the time it feels like there's nowhere to go.

It all feels harum-scarum like going through a
pandemonium,
As I restore my equilibrium;
I try not to worry as it's become the norm of the
millenium.
I hope all of this yet brings the continuum,
And would help to discover my spectrum enabling
momentum.

19. Present is the Present

Humans keep revisiting the past.
Or keep worrying about the future anxiously.
Little did we know that advancement in the world will
lead us to live unhappily in this rapidly growing world.
Here, we are so engrossed in achieving goals and desires
that we have forgotten to live in the present!

It's a sad state of affairs for all of us.
We are not only prone to myriad physical health and
mental health issues because of this.
But we are also neglecting to live in contentment.

Seems it's taking us nowhere in reality.
Sometimes we live in past and sometimes in future but
expect to be happy and content in the present.
Let's remember that...
Past is defunct and future is unforeseeable but present is
the only present we have.

20. Connect Your Dots

They say work hard and you'll succeed,
But they don't emphasize enough on knowing that,
Accepting and putting yourself together to be one.
Acknowledging all of your parts - good, bad and ugly is
of paramount importance.

Finding the bad and ugly parts of yourself is most
difficult.
Once you find it, it's difficult to come to terms with it.
After you find those fragments, it takes time to process
it.
Then it's followed by unvented & unhealed emotions
which come crawling back.

You feel as scared as witnessing a ghost,
It clouds your senses.
It feels as though your inner being is like a dilapidated
building which is in desperate need of repair.
You got to face those.

These are your inner demons.
You don't get rid of inner demons.
You embrace them and make peace with them.
These are charred fragments of your wholeness.
It burns like a wildfire and like a slow death.

But remember, in order to put yourself together,
You will have to connect to all your sides.
Only then you'll see the path of success.
At that point, you'll usher yourself to the path of success.
Just like you connect dots to form a straight line,
Connect your dots to reach to the destination.

21. You

You are like that comfortable warm cloth
that feels fit only after a 100 wears.
Not everyone is that patient.
Not everyone will get you.
Not everyone is meant to understand you.
Only the few chosen ones will..
You have the depth and layers,
That needs patience to unravel;
Only the bravest and strongest can be patient.
Hence, it takes time to find those
That thrive with you and resonate similarly.
Until you find them on your wavelength,
You keep circumnavigating,
Scouting innermost layers and peeling them off.
Realizing the way out was inward...
That shine of yours,
That light you bring around,
Came at a cost..
That not everyone will understand and believe,
That some will shrug off,

You are like that candle that had to burn and purge
To illuminate others,
You were their beacon of light,
Your innocent soul feels happy to see them reach their
destination;
Whilst you lost steer & were directionless to your own...
You still never gave up for yourself.
You have lived the darkest of nightmares to reach your
destination
Now it's time to live the daydreams
Now its time to light up your own world
Now it's time to feel every nerve come alive
Now it's time to finally live for yourself
Now it's time to be YOU